나는 우리 엄마를 사랑해요
I LOVE MY MOM

지은이: 셸리 애드몬트

삽화: 소날 고얄, 수밋 사쿠자

www.sachildrensbooks.com

Copyright©2014 by Inna Nusinsky Shmuilov

innans@gmail.com

All rights reserved. No part of this book may be reproduced in any form or by any electronic or mechanical means, including information storage and retrieval systems, without written permission from the publisher or author, except in the case of a reviewer, who may quote brief passages embodied in critical articles or in a review.

모든 권한을 보유합니다

First edition, 2016

Translated from English by Soo Min Rhee

번역: 이수민

I Love My Mom (Korean English Bilingual Edition)/ Shelley Admont

ISBN: 978-1-77268-364-6 paperback

ISBN: 978-1-77268-602-9 hardcover

ISBN: 978-1-77268-363-9 eBook

Please note that the Korean and English versions of the story have been written to be as close as possible. However, in some cases they differ in order to accommodate nuances and fluidity of each language.

Although the author and the publisher have made every effort to ensure the accuracy and completeness of information contained in this book, we assume no responsibility for errors , inaccuracies, omission, inconsistency, or consequences from such information.

내가 가장 사랑하는 사람들에게
for those I love the most

내일은 엄마의 생일이에요. 아기 토끼 지미와 지미의 형들은 방에서 속닥거렸어요.
Tomorrow was Mom's birthday. The little bunny Jimmy and his two older brothers were whispering in their room.

"곰곰이 한 번 생각해 보자," 큰 형이 말했어요. "엄마 생일 선물은 특별해야해."
"Let's think," said the middle brother. "The present for Mom should be very special."

"지미야, 넌 항상 좋은 아이디어를 갖고 있잖아," 작은 형이 말했어요. "어떻게 생각해?"
"Jimmy, you always have good ideas," added the oldest brother. "What do you think?"

"음…" 지미는 곰곰이 생각하기 시작했어요. 그러다 갑자기 소리질렀어요. "내가 제일 좋아하는 장남감을 드릴 수 있는데 -- 기차 장난감 말이야!" 지미는 장난감 상자에서 기차를 꺼내서 형들에게 보여줬어요.

"Ahm…" Jimmy started thinking hard. Suddenly he exclaimed, "I can give her my favorite toy — my train!" He took the train out of the toy box and showed it to his brothers.

"내 생각에 엄마는 네 기차를 원하지 않으실 것 같은데." 큰 형이 말했어요. "다른 아이디어가 필요해. 엄마가 진짜 좋아하실 만한 것으로."

"I don't think Mom likes trains," said the oldest brother. "We need another idea. Something that she will really like."

"아, 나한테 좋은 생각이 하나 있어," 작은 형이 기쁜 마음으로 소리를 질렀어요. "선물로 책을 드리자."
"Oh, I have one," screamed the middle brother happily. "We can give her a book."

"책? 엄마에게 완벽한 선물이야." 큰 형이 대답했어요. "엄마는 책을 진짜 좋아하셔!"
"A book? It's a perfect gift for Mom," replied the oldest brother.

"그래, 내가 가장 좋아하는 책을 드리자," 작은 형이 책장에 다가가며 말했어요.
"Yes, we can give her my favorite book," said the middle brother as he approached the bookshelf.

"하지만 엄마는 미스테리 책을 좋아하신단 말이야," 지미가 슬프게 말했어요. "이건 어린이 책이잖아."
"But Mom likes mystery books," said Jimmy sadly, "and this book is for kids."

"네 말이 옳은 것 같아," 작은 형이 동의했어요.
"우리 어떻게 해야하지?"
"I guess you're right," agreed his middle brother. "What should we do?"

세 토끼 형제들은 앉아서 조용히 생각해 보았어요. 그러자 큰 형이 말했어요.

The three bunny brothers were sitting and thinking quietly, until the oldest brother finally said,

"내가 생각할 수 있는 것은 딱 한가지야. 우리가 혼자 할 수 있는 것, 이를테면 카드 같은 것 말이야."

"There is only one thing that I can think of. Something that we can do by ourselves, like a card."

"하트모양을 아주 많이 그리자," 작은 형이 말했어요.

"We can draw millions of millions of hearts and kisses," said the middle brother.

"우리가 엄마를 얼마나 사랑하는지 보여 주는거야," 큰 형이 말했어요.

"And tell Mom how much we love her," added the oldest brother.

모두들 신나서 카드를 만들기 시작했어요.
They all became very excited and started to work.

세 토끼는 자르고 붙이고 접고, 또 색칠하며 아주 열심히 만들었어요.
Three bunnies worked very hard. They cut and glued, folded and painted.

지미와 작은 형은 하트와 뽀뽀 모양을 그렸어요. 다 만든 후, 그들은 더 많은 하트와 뽀뽀 모양을 카드에 그렸어요.
Jimmy and his middle brother drew hearts and kisses. When they finished, they added more hearts and even more kisses.

그런 뒤에, 큰 형이 글씨를 크게 썼어요:
Then the oldest brother wrote in large letters:

"엄마, 생일을 축하드려요! 아주 많이 많이 사랑해요. 엄마 아들들이."
"Happy birthday, Mommy! We love you soooooooo much. Your kids."

드디어 생일 카드가 완성이 되었어요. 지미는 미소를 지었어요.
Finally, the card was ready. Jimmy smiled.

"엄마가 분명히 좋아하실 거야," 그가 더러운 손을 바지에 문질러대며 말했어요.
"I'm sure Mom will like it," he said, wiping his dirty hands on his pants.

"지미, 지금 뭐하는거야?" 큰 형이 소리질렀어요. "네 손이 페인트랑 풀로 범벅인 것이 안보여?"
"Jimmy," screamed the oldest brother. "Don't you see your hands are covered in paint and glue?"

"아…" 지미가 말했어요. "몰랐어 형, 미안해!"
"Oh, oh…" said Jimmy. "I didn't notice. Sorry!"

"이제 엄마가 생일날 빨래를 하셔야 하잖아," 큰 형이 지미를 엄하게 쳐다보며 말했어요.
"Now Mom has to do laundry on her own birthday," added the oldest brother, looking at Jimmy strictly.

"아니야! 그렇게 되지 않도록 할게!" 지미가 큰소리 쳤어요. "내가 스스로 빨래를 할게." 지미는 화장실로 향했어요.
"No way! I won't let this happen!" exclaimed Jimmy. "I'll wash my pants myself." He headed into the bathroom.

세 형제들은 지미의 바지에 묻은 페인트와 풀을 함께 씻어내고 마를 수 있도록 바지를 걸어놨어요.
Together they washed all the paint and glue from the pants and hung them to dry.

방으로 돌아오는 길에 지미는 거실을 힐끗 쳐다보며 엄마가 있는지 확인했어요.
On the way back to their room, Jimmy gave a quick glance into living room and saw their Mom there.

"저기를 봐, 엄마가 지금 소파에서 주무시고 계셔," 지미가 형들에게 속삭였어요.
"Look, Mom is sleeping on the couch," whispered Jimmy to his brothers.

"내 이불을 가지고 올게," 방으로 달려가며 큰 형이 말했어요.
"I'll bring my blanket," said the older brother who ran back to their room.

지미는 서서 엄마가 주무시고 있는 걸 쳐다봤어요. 그 순간 엄마에게 딱 좋은 선물이 무엇인지 깨달았어요. 지미는 미소를 지었어요.

Jimmy was standing and looking at his Mom sleeping. In that moment he realized what the perfect gift for their Mom should be. He smiled.

"좋은 생각이 하나 있어!" 큰 형이 이불을 가지고 올때 지미가 말했어요.

"I have an idea!" said Jimmy when the oldest brother came back with the blanket.

지미가 형들에게 무언가를 속삭였고, 세 토끼들 모두 다 미소를 환하게 지으며 고개를 끄덕였어요.

He whispered something to his brothers and all three bunnies nodded their heads, smiling widely.

세 형제는 조용히 엄마 곁으로 다가가 이불을 덮어드렸어요.
Quietly they approached the couch and covered their Mom with the blanket.

모두 다 엄마에게 다정하게 뽀뽀를 하고 "엄마, 사랑해요," 라고 속삭였어요.
Each of them kissed her gently and whispered, "We love you, Mommy."

엄마가 눈을 떴어요. "나도 너희들을 사랑한단다," 라고 말하며 웃으면서 아들들을 안아 주었어요.
Mom opened her eyes. "Oh, I love you too," she said, smiling and hugging her sons.

다음날 아침, 세 토끼 형제들은 엄마에게 깜짝 선물을 준비하기 위해 아주 일찍 일어났어요.

The next morning, the three bunny brothers woke up very early to prepare their surprise present for Mom.

이빨을 닦고, 이불을 완벽하게 정리하며 장난감이 제자리에 있는지 확인했어요.

They brushed their teeth, made their beds perfectly and checked that all the toys were in place.

그런 다음, 먼지를 털고 바닥을 닦기 위해 거실로 갔어요.

After that, they headed to the living room to clean the dust and wash the floor.

다음으로 세 형제들은 부엌으로 왔어요.
Next, they came into the kitchen.

"난 엄마가 제일 좋아하는 딸기잼을 얹은 토스트를 준비할게," 큰 형이 말했어요. "지미야, 너는 생과일 오렌지 주스를 만들어 드릴래?"
"I'll prepare Mom's favorite toasts with strawberry jam," said the oldest brother, "and you, Jimmy, can make her fresh orange juice."

"난 정원에서 꽃을 따서 올게," 밖으로 나가며 작은 형이 말했어요.
"I'll bring some flowers from the garden," said the middle brother who went out the door.

아침 식사가 준비되었을때 토끼들은 설거지를 하고 꽃이랑 풍선을 가지고 부엌을 꾸몄어요.
When breakfast was ready, the bunnies washed all the dishes and decorated the kitchen with flowers and balloons.

행복한 토끼 형제들은 생일 카드, 꽃, 그리고 방금 막 만든 아침을 가지고 엄마와 아빠 방으로 들어갔어요.
The happy bunny brothers entered Mom and Dad's room holding the birthday card, the flowers and the fresh breakfast.

엄마는 침대 위에 앉아 있었어요. 아들들이 방으로 들어오며 "생일을 축하드립니다" 노래를 부르자 미소를 지었어요.
Mom was sitting on the bed. She smiled as she heard her sons singing "Happy Birthday," while they entered the room.

"엄마 사랑해요," 다 함께 소리질렀어요.
"We love you, Mom," they screamed all together.

"나도 너희들을 모두 사랑한단다," 엄마가 아들들에게 뽀뽀하며 말했어요. "오늘은 내 인생에서 최고의 생일이야!"
"I love you all too," said Mom, kissing all her sons. "It's my best birthday ever!"

"아직 다 안보셨어요," 지미가 형들에게 윙크를 하며 말했어요. "주방이랑 거실을 한번 보세요!"

"You haven't seen everything yet," said Jimmy with a wink to his brothers. **"You should check the kitchen and the living room!"**

MAR -- 2020

Lightning Source UK Ltd.
Milton Keynes UK
UKHW052202270819
348701UK00006B/250/P

9 781772 683646